Catherine the Great

Elizabeth Raum

Raintree

Chicago, Illinois

HEINEMANN·RAINTREE

TO ORDER:

☎ Phone Customer Service **888-454-2279**

💻 Visit **www.heinemannraintree.com** to browse our catalog and order online.

© 2009 Raintree
a division of Pearson Inc.
Chicago, Illinois

Editorial: Louise Galpine, Diyan Leake, and Kristen Truhlar
Design: Jennifer Lacki, Kim Miracle, and Betsy Wernert
Illustrations: Mapping Specialists
Picture Research: Mica Brancic
Production: Vicki Fitzgerald

Originated by Modern Age
Printed and bound in China by Leo Paper Group

ISBN-13: 978-1-4109-3221-1 (hc)
ISBN-10: 1-4109-3221-4 (hc)

13 12 11 10 09
10 9 8 7 6 5 4 3 2 1

Library of Congress Cataloging-in-Publication Data
Raum, Elizabeth.
 Catherine the Great / Elizabeth Raum.
  p. cm. -- (Great women leaders)
 Includes bibliographical references and index.
 ISBN 978-1-4109-3221-1 (hc)
 1. Catherine II, Empress of Russia, 1729-1796--Juvenile literature. 2. Empresses--Russia--Biography--Juvenile literature. 3. Russia--History--Catherine II, 1762-1796--Juvenile literature. I. Title.
 DK170.R38 2008
 947'.063092--dc22
 [B]
                              2007049819

Acknowledgments
The author and publishers are grateful to the following for permission to reproduce copyright material: © Alamy pp. **17** (CuboImages srl), **29** (Mary Evans Picture Library); © Corbis pp. **5** (The Art Archive), **6**, **8** (Archivo Iconograficao, S.A.), **10** (dpa/epd-Bild Norbert Neetz), **16** (The Art Archive), **23** (Reproduced by permission of The State Hermitage Museum, St. Petersburg, Russia), **27** bottom (Wolfgang Kaehler), **33** (Adam Woolfitt), **37** (Bettmann), **41** (Michel Setboun), **45** (Yogi, Inc.); © Getty Images p. **36** (National Geographic/Cary Wolinsky); © The Bridgeman Art Library pp. **9** (Private Collection, Paul Freeman), **11** (Bildarchiv Steffens), **12** (Hermitage, St. Petersburg, Russia), **14** (Tsarskoye Selo, St. Petersburg, Russia), **18** (Private Collection, Photo © Christie's Images), **19** (Kremlin Museums, Moscow, Russia), **21** (© Odessa Fina Arts Museum, Ukraine), **22** (Vladimir Art Museum, Russia), **24** (Kremlin Museums, Moscow, Russia), **27** top (State Russian Museum, St. Petersburg, Russia), **30** (Hermitage, St. Petersburg, Russia), **31** (Tretyakov Gallery, Moscow, Russia), **35** (Private Collection, © Look and Learn), **43** (Central Naval Museum, St. Petersburg Russia), **44** (Hermitage, St. Petersburg, Russia), **47** (Hermitage, St. Petersburg, Russia); © The State Hermitage Museum, St. Petersburg pp. **25**, **32**, **38**.

Cover photograph reproduced with the permission of © The Art Archive (Russian Historical Museum Moscow/ Alfredo Dagli Orti).

The publishers would like to thank Nancy Harris for her assistance in the preparation of this book.

Every effort has been made to contact copyright holders of any material reproduced in this book. Any omissions will be rectified in subsequent printings if notice is given to the publisher.

Disclaimer
All the Internet addresses (URLs) given in this book were valid at the time of going to press. However, due to the dynamic nature of the Internet, some addresses may have changed, or sites may have changed or ceased to exist since publication. While the author and publisher regret any inconvenience this may cause readers, no responsibility for any such changes can be accepted by either the author or the publisher.

CONTENTS

Some words are shown in bold, **like this**. You can find out what they mean by looking in the glossary.

CATHERINE, EMPRESS OF RUSSIA

From 1762 to 1796, Catherine the Great was the most powerful woman in the world. As empress of Russia, she ruled a vast land that extended across both Europe and Asia. During the 34 years that Catherine was Russia's ruler, she made life and death decisions on a daily basis.

A most unusual woman

Today many women hold powerful positions in government and business. But that was not true when Catherine lived. During the 1700s, most women spent their lives at home, as wives and mothers, or as servants. School was for boys only. Most women could not read or write. Women may have advised their husbands, but only in private. They rarely spoke out in public.

However, when Catherine spoke, people did as she said. Catherine was an intelligent and determined woman who became a key decision-maker and world leader. Catherine spoke German, French, and Russian. She read encyclopedias, books about government and **philosophy**, poetry, and novels. She wrote daily, and her writing included reports, plays, and her **memoirs** (the story of her life). During the **reign** of Catherine the Great, Russia became a strong nation that earned the respect of other European countries.

An impressive reign

In her memoirs Catherine claimed that under her rule Russia built 144 new cities, won 78 military victories, and signed 30 treaties (agreements) with other nations. She also noted that 123 laws were made to improve life for the people of Russia.

A strange twist

Catherine was an unlikely leader for Russia: she was a woman in a time when most leaders were men, and she was not Russian. Her name was not Catherine, either. It was Sophia. She was a German princess from an unknown family. Her story is the story of someone who knew what she wanted and was determined to reach her goals.

This painting shows Catherine the Great in 1770. In public she wore precious jewels and expensive fabrics.

PRINCESS SOPHIE

On April 21, 1729, Sophia Augusta Fredericka (who was known as Sophie as a child) was born in the German-speaking town of Stettin in the kingdom of Prussia. Her parents, Prince Christian Augustus and Princess Johanna Elizabeth, had hoped for a son. They were disappointed to learn that the baby was a girl. They sent her to the nursery with a nursemaid.

Family ties

Sophie's parents were not wealthy or powerful. Like many princes of the time, Prince Christian Augustus had a royal title, but no kingdom. His **principality**, Anhalt-Zerbst, had little wealth or influence. Even so, Prince Christian Augustus had the right to be called a prince. His children would be princes and princesses.

Sophie's father was a major-general in the Prussian Army and governor of Stettin, a city in the kingdom of Prussia. Prussia was made up of many smaller regions called principalities. Each principality was ruled by a prince who reported to the king of Prussia. The nation of Germany did not exist until 1871. Before that, there were various German-speaking kingdoms, like the kingdom of Prussia.

Sophie's father was governor of Stettin, a town in Prussia.

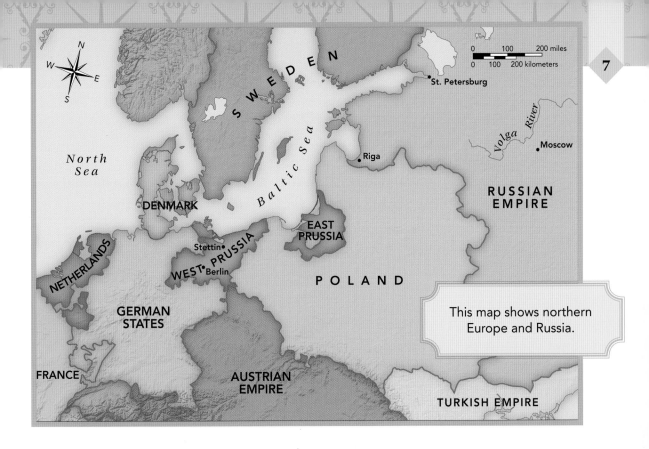

This map shows northern Europe and Russia.

Prince Christian Augustus was loyal, religious, and thrifty. He was 37 years old when he married Johanna Elizabeth, who was only 15. Their families had arranged for the two to marry. Before they married, they barely knew each other.

Sophie's mother wanted more for her children than useless titles and a drafty castle. She was distantly related to the Swedish royal family. If she had a son, he might someday become the king of Sweden. She would have to arrange a good marriage for her daughter.

Arranged marriage

Royal parents often arranged their children's marriages when the children were quite young. Being "in love" was not important. Often the couple did not meet until the wedding. Sometimes the marriage created a partnership between nations or kingdoms. Sometimes parents wanted to make sure that their child married someone with money and power. Many times the marriages worked out well because the husband and wife shared similar backgrounds and values.

Learning to be a princess

Sophie learned how to behave at **court**. When her mother entertained other women, little Sophie **curtsied** and kissed the hems of the women's dresses. Royal children dressed like adults. At parties Sophie wore a ball gown with a hoop skirt. A maid powdered her hair in the style of the day.

This painting from the mid-1700s shows royal children dressed in the fashions of adults.

Scabby skin and a bent spine

As a child, Sophie suffered from a common skin infection called impetigo. She developed itchy, sore blisters that oozed and crusted over. Several times her nurse shaved Sophie's long hair to give the sores on her head the air they needed to heal. At age seven, Sophie nearly died of pleurisy, a lung disease that causes coughing and pain when breathing. Her doctors also noticed that her spine was growing crooked. Sophie later wrote, "My spine made a zigzag." She wore a back brace. By the time she was 11, her back was straight, and she returned to full health.

Tomboy

Sophie never liked to play with dolls. Sophie was a member of the **nobility**, and noble children usually played with other noble children. However, Sophie's parents allowed her to invite the children of local merchants to the castle for rough and tumble games. She quickly became their leader. Once she had learned to shoot a gun, she enjoyed bird hunting. She also enjoyed horseback riding.

This soup plate belonged to Sophie's parents. It is decorated with the **coat-of-arms** of Christian Augustus, prince of Anhalt-Zerbst.

Meeting the king

When Sophie was four years old she met the king of Prussia, Frederick William I, who ruled the entire nation. Sophie was expected to kiss the hem of the king's coat. But she refused, claiming that she could not reach it. The king laughed and called her rude.

Lessons to learn

Sophie did not attend school. Teachers came to the castle. Her **governess**, Babet Cardel, taught her French, the language of royalty. Everyone at **court** spoke French. Other teachers came to the castle and taught Sophie German, dancing, and music. She loved everything but music, which she never enjoyed.

Sophie's father was a **devout Lutheran**. He believed the teachings of Martin Luther (1483–1546), who in 1517 had led the **Reformation** that divided the Christian church into **Catholic** and **Protestant**. Sophie did not get along well with her religion teacher, who was a Lutheran pastor. Her constant questions disturbed him, but he admitted she was well-behaved and capable.

Martin Luther, a priest, rebelled against the teachings of the Catholic church and established the Lutheran faith. Many in Germany, including Sophie's father, were Lutheran.

A real princess

Because of her skin problems and bent spine, Sophie thought of herself as ugly. But as she turned 10, she began to feel more attractive. She was extremely thin and quite tall. She had dark blue eyes, a long nose, and a pointed chin. When she looked in a mirror, she began to imagine herself as a queen.

She went with her parents to visit other royal families. She realized that she was not like the children she played with in Stettin. She was destined for a grander life, a royal life.

Surviving in the 18th century

Sophie's mother gave birth to two sons and three daughters. Two girls died in infancy. A brother died at age 12. Only Sophie and her youngest brother lived to adulthood. At this time, accidents and disease killed many children, and there were few effective medical treatments. In the 1700s, 300–400 of every 1,000 babies born did not live beyond age one. Worldwide, the average person lived to be about 24 years old in 1796, the year that Sophie died.

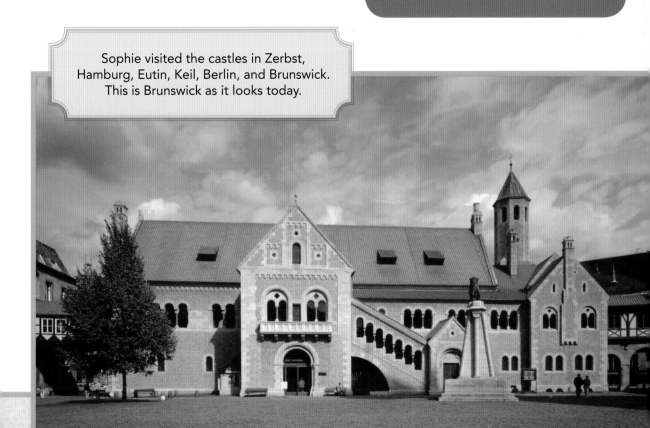

Sophie visited the castles in Zerbst, Hamburg, Eutin, Keil, Berlin, and Brunswick. This is Brunswick as it looks today.

DREAMS OF RUSSIA

In 1739 at a party in Kiel, Sophie met Prince Karl Peter Ulrich, who lived in Holstein, a state in Prussia. Karl Peter was 11 and Sophie was 10. The boy was small and sickly. He was not good at conversation. Sophie realized quickly that the prince, who was known as Peter, did not read. All he cared about was playing soldier.

Prince Karl Peter Ulrich

Peter was the son of Empress Elizabeth's sister, Anna, and Karl Friedrich, a German **duke**. Peter's mother died when he was three months old. He was 11 when his father died. Peter was small for his age, often sick, and shy. Empress Elizabeth had never met her nephew until he arrived in Russia in 1742, when she began to look after him.

She overheard the adults say that he was likely to become king of either Sweden or Russia. If this boy became a king, his wife would be a queen. Years later Sophie wrote about how that idea inspired her. She began to picture herself married to this unusual boy.

By the time Sophie was 11 or 12, she began to imagine herself as a queen. This portrait shows a confident, elegantly dressed Sophie.

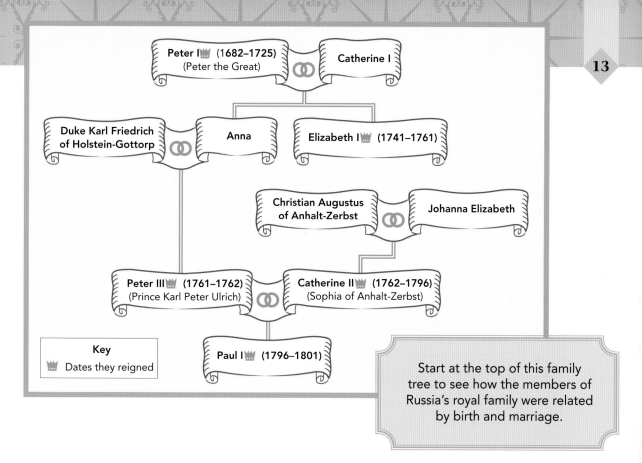

Peter I 👑 (1682–1725)
(Peter the Great)

Catherine I

Duke Karl Friedrich
of Holstein-Gottorp

Anna

Elizabeth I 👑 (1741–1761)

Christian Augustus
of Anhalt-Zerbst

Johanna Elizabeth

Peter III 👑 (1761–1762)
(Prince Karl Peter Ulrich)

Catherine II 👑 (1762–1796)
(Sophia of Anhalt-Zerbst)

Key
👑 Dates they reigned

Paul I 👑 (1796–1801)

Start at the top of this family tree to see how the members of Russia's royal family were related by birth and marriage.

Looking to Russia

In December of 1741, Johanna learned that Russia had a new leader, Elizabeth, daughter of Peter the Great. A month later Elizabeth chose Prince Karl Peter Ulrich, her nephew, to take over the Russian throne when she died. This was the same boy Sophie had met in Kiel.

Johanna sent congratulations to the new empress. After all, Elizabeth had once been engaged to Johanna's brother, Karl Augustus. Elizabeth sent a kind note back to Johanna. She also sent a portrait of herself in a frame set with diamonds.

Johanna was thrilled. Even though Karl Augustus died before the wedding took place, Elizabeth had not forgotten him or his family. Elizabeth's note and portrait gave Johanna hope that a marriage between Sophie and Peter was possible. Sophie was still a child, but it would take time to arrange a proper marriage.

This portrait of Empress Elizabeth was painted about the time she first contacted Sophie's mother, Johanna. At the time all portraits were paintings because the camera had not been invented.

A portrait in return

Johanna sent Sophie to Berlin to have her portrait painted. Once it was done, Johanna sent the painting to Elizabeth in Russia. Johanna and Sophie waited nervously to see if Elizabeth would decide that Sophie was a good match for her nephew, Peter.

Waiting for word

Weeks and months passed with no word from Russia. Sophie attended balls, parties, concerts, and hunting events with her mother. People began to take an interest in the well-spoken, self-confident teenager. Finally, on New Year's Day 1744, Empress Elizabeth sent a letter inviting Johanna and Sophie to Russia.

The king checks in

Only two hours later another letter arrived. It was from Frederick II, king of Prussia. To everyone's surprise, he already knew about the invitation from Russia. He was eager for Sophie to marry Peter, now known as Grand Duke Peter of Russia. The king hoped the marriage would bring Prussia and Russia closer together.

To go to Russia or not?

Sophie's father thought Russia was too far from Prussia. Just as Johanna had feared, he did not want Sophie to marry into the Russian royal family. He knew that Sophie's life would not be easy in Russia. If Sophie angered Empress Elizabeth, she might end up in prison. Others had. Sophie would have to give up her **Lutheran** faith to become **Russian Orthodox**, the state religion of Russia. Her father said no.

No one thought to ask Sophie what she wanted. For three days, she listened to her parents argue over her future. But Sophie finally spoke up. She told her mother that she wanted to go to Russia. Together they convinced Sophie's father that going to Russia was a wise decision.

Empress Elizabeth insisted that Sophie and her mother come alone. Sophie's father was not invited. They were not to tell anyone about the trip. If Elizabeth approved of Sophie, then she would make the announcement.

Frederick II lived in an elegant palace in Berlin. Sophie had to borrow a fancy gown before dining with the king.

First stop: Berlin

On January 10, 1744, Sophie and her parents left for Berlin to meet with Frederick II, king of Prussia. The king wanted to meet 14-year-old Sophie before she left for Russia in order to judge her chances of pleasing the Russian **court**. The king seated Sophie at his own table and talked with her throughout the banquet.

Across the frozen north

On January 16, 1744, Sophie bid farewell to her father before setting out for Russia with her mother. They traveled in secret, under false names. Four carriages held the women, their servants, and their baggage. A small stove in the carriage and heaps of furs barely kept them warm in the bitter cold weather. At night they stopped at inns. If the bedrooms were unheated, everyone crowded into the innkeeper's private room and slept with his family, children, dogs, chickens, and other livestock. After three terrible weeks they reached Russia.

Russian welcome

When they reached the city of Riga, cannon fire greeted them. They transferred to an elegant sleigh for the ride to the castle. When Sophie attended dinner, trumpets saluted her, and everyone bowed their heads in respect. She was astounded and delighted by the warm Russian welcome.

After a night in Riga, Sophie and Johanna traveled to St. Petersburg in a covered sleigh called a kibitka. It was decorated with scarlet curtains trimmed in silver. Sophie reclined on a feather bed covered with furs and listened to the jingle of sleigh bells as she glided across the frozen plains.

Nervousness

Shortly after leaving Riga, Sophie and her mother reached St. Petersburg. They stayed at the Winter Palace. Sophie toured St. Petersburg, admiring its frozen beauty. Her mother loved court life. Sophie wanted to fit in, but she did not have the right clothes. She worried that the nobles in St. Petersburg did not approve of her.

When they arrived at St. Petersburg, Sophie and her mother stayed at the Winter Palace.

BECOMING RUSSIAN

A few weeks later, Sophie and her mother traveled to Moscow to meet Grand **Duke** Peter and his aunt, Empress Elizabeth. They traveled day and night, stopping only to eat. Finally, when they were four hours from Moscow, they changed into their best clothes and prepared to meet the empress.

Grand Duke Peter greeted them. He was not as handsome as Catherine remembered. In fact, she thought him ugly. But he was friendly and clearly pleased to see her. Sixteen-year-old Peter welcomed Sophie and her mother in German. Then he took them to meet Empress Elizabeth.

When Sophie arrived at Moscow's Kremlin Palace, it probably looked similar to the scene in this painting.

The Order of St. Catherine was a medal given to women.

The empress

Elizabeth was beautiful. She wore diamond bracelets and necklaces. More diamonds were woven into her hair. Even her gown sparkled with diamonds. Sophie was overwhelmed, but she managed to **curtsy** gracefully.

Elizabeth seemed impressed with the young princess. The very next day, Elizabeth awarded Sophie and Johanna the Order of St. Catherine, a medal established to honor Elizabeth's mother. It was a sign of approval.

First impressions

Sophie and Peter spent much time together, laughing and playing silly games. Peter enjoyed talking with Sophie in German. Peter so loved his native Prussia that he refused to learn Russian. Sophie considered such rebellion childish. She was shocked that he still played with toy soldiers. She realized she would not marry for love, but rather for power.

Empress Elizabeth

Elizabeth Petrova was the second daughter of Russia's most famous leader, Peter the Great. She seized control of the Russian government in 1741, claiming the throne for herself. Her young nephew, Ivan VI, was the rightful king, but Elizabeth put him in jail so she could take over. Elizabeth was poorly educated, but shrewd (clever). During her 20 years as empress, she chose advisors who helped Russia advance in military and political power. A jealous and **vain** woman, she was rumored to own over 15,000 dresses and 5,000 pairs of shoes.

Eager student

Sophie learned the Russian language and the ways of the Russian **court** quickly. She was so determined to master Russian that she begged her teacher to continue lessons long after class was over. She got up at night to study in the freezing palace. When Sophie caught a cold, Johanna tried to hide her illness. But it developed into **pneumonia**. Sophie was near death. She asked to speak to a **Russian Orthodox** priest. It was a decision that earned her Elizabeth's loyalty. The entire court soon learned of Sophie's determination to learn Russian and of her respect for the Russian Orthodox faith.

Engaged

By her 15th birthday, April 21, 1744, Sophie had recovered enough to join 40 guests at a birthday dinner. In the days that followed, Sophie returned to her studies.

On June 28, 1744, Sophie **converted** to the Russian Orthodox faith. During a service in the royal chapel, Sophie read aloud over 50 pages in Russian. Empress Elizabeth cried during the moving ceremony. As a sign that Sophie was no longer a German or a **Lutheran**, she took a new name. Elizabeth suggested the name Catherine. This was the name of Elizabeth's mother.

All that shimmers is not gold

The 18th-century Russian palaces looked beautiful from a distance, but up close they were falling apart and drafty. The Kremlin's marble walls were actually made of bricks painted white. Roofs leaked and doors hung crooked. The stairs were unsafe and in danger of collapse. The heating system consisted of old stoves that belched smoke. Fires were a constant hazard in the palace and throughout the city.

Early the next morning, Elizabeth announced Catherine and Peter's engagement. The young couple exchanged rings in an exhausting four-hour ceremony. Everyone stood, and by the end Catherine's legs were numb.

Catherine's new title was "Grand Duchess of Russia." Empress Elizabeth gave the young couple gifts of jewels and money. Everyone attended a ball in their honor.

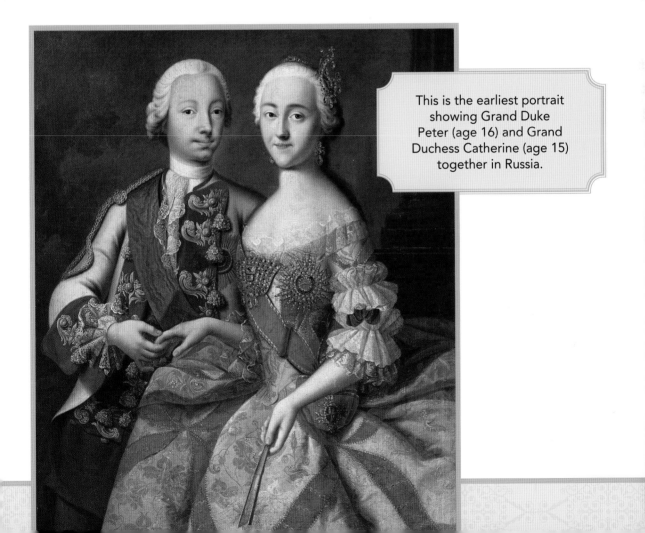

This is the earliest portrait showing Grand Duke Peter (age 16) and Grand Duchess Catherine (age 15) together in Russia.

Celebrating

After the engagement, Elizabeth showered Catherine with gifts and arranged parties and outings. Elizabeth surrounded Catherine with young and cheerful **ladies-in-waiting**, **grooms**, and various servants who would amuse and entertain her.

The onion domes of the cathedral appear in the center of this painting of Kiev. Today Kiev, located 470 miles (750 kilometers) from Moscow, is the capital city of the Ukraine.

In August 1744, Catherine and Peter accompanied Elizabeth to Kiev, Russia's oldest and holiest city. Catherine was touched by the respect the Russian people showed their empress. Catherine did not normally see common Russian people. In Kiev she saw them— rich and poor, old and young, male and female—and wanted to learn more about them and their way of life.

Smallpox strikes

In December of 1744, Peter came down with **smallpox**. Catherine wanted to stay with him and nurse him back to health, but her mother said no. Catherine might catch the disease, too. So Catherine and her mother left Peter in the care of Empress Elizabeth, who remained with him throughout his illness.

Elizabeth risked illness and the scars of smallpox by staying at Peter's side. Elizabeth was a vain woman who put her looks above most other concerns. Catherine admired Elizabeth's courage and concern for her nephew.

Peter recovered, but his face was scarred. Catherine was not marrying Peter for his looks or his personality, but for his crown. Wedding planning continued.

When Catherine saw the beautiful **Russian Orthodox** icons (religious images) at Kiev, she wrote,

"I have never been more impressed in my life than I was by the extraordinary splendor of this church in which all the images are covered with gold, silver, and jewels."

A Time to Marry

The wedding, which took place on August 21, 1745, lasted several hours. A banquet and a ball followed. At nine o'clock, the party ended, and Catherine went to her room. She waited there for Peter, but he partied late into the night with friends.

Catherine's wedding dress

For the wedding, Catherine wore her dark hair long and unpowdered. Her white dress was decorated with silver embroidery. The floor-length dress had a wide skirt that emphasized Catherine's tiny waist. She wore a huge cloak of silver lace and a heavy gold tiara. Pearls, diamonds, and precious jewels completed her outfit. Peter wore a suit of the same silver embroidery and he had an equal number of jewels.

Catherine and Peter rode to their wedding in a golden carriage drawn by eight white horses. There were 120 other carriages in the wedding parade. This carriage, built for Catherine, is now in the Kremlin Museum.

Alone

A month after the wedding, Elizabeth ordered Johanna, Catherine's mother, to leave Russia. Johanna had been working behind the scenes to expand Prussian influence. Elizabeth no longer trusted her. Catherine found herself, at 16, alone in a foreign land and married to a man she did not even like. She read for hours each day, preparing for the day when she would be empress. She enjoyed horseback riding and would often leave the palace early in the morning to ride or go bird hunting.

Peter's pranks

Peter remained childish. He organized a puppet theater and played soldier. He drank too much and laughed too loudly. One day, Peter drilled a hole in the wall that faced Elizabeth's room. He watched as she ate and entertained friends. Then he invited others, including Catherine, to join him. When Elizabeth found out, she was furious. She sent away many of Peter's friends. Peter turned to Catherine for comfort, but they still were not close.

Soon after the wedding, Catherine's mother (above) was ordered to leave Russia.

Elizabeth was unmarried—she would never have children—so she expected Peter and Catherine to produce a son. A son would carry on the royal line established by Elizabeth's father, Peter the Great. Five years passed, then six, seven, and eight. Catherine and Peter still did not have a child.

A jealous empress

As Catherine grew more beautiful, the aging Elizabeth became jealous. Jealousy made Elizabeth dangerous. Catherine found herself surrounded by spies who reported her every word and deed to Elizabeth. So Catherine learned how to survive the dangers of **court**. She gave gifts to those who could help her, found ways to please Elizabeth, and learned all that she could about Russia and its politics. Catherine ordered books from abroad and began writing instructions to herself about how to govern when she became empress of Russia.

A son at last

On September 20, 1754, nine years after her wedding, Catherine gave birth to a son. Empress Elizabeth named him Paul and whisked him away to her apartments. As empress, Elizabeth could do as she pleased. Naming and claiming the child was what she wanted to do. Even though Catherine sobbed with loneliness, no one came to her aid.

It was six weeks before Catherine saw her infant son again. "I found him very beautiful," she wrote in her **memoirs**, "and the sight of him raised my spirits a little." After Catherine's brief glimpse, Elizabeth took the baby away again. She raised him as if he were her own son.

Paul was about seven when this portrait was painted.

Who was Paul?

Some claimed that Paul was not Peter's son, but the son of a young **courtier** named Sergei Saltykov. Catherine and Sergei became friends, and it is quite possible that Paul was their son. Catherine never admitted this, but she hinted that Paul was not Peter's child. It didn't seem to matter to Elizabeth. She was pleased to claim Paul as heir to the Russian throne.

Paul was born in the Summer Palace in St. Petersburg.

Elizabeth's plan for the future

Empress Elizabeth, who was 44 when Paul was born, hoped to make him emperor after her death, instead of Peter and Catherine. Elizabeth no longer trusted Peter or Catherine. It was no secret that the Russian people did not like Peter, either. He supported Frederick II of Prussia, even though Russia was at war with the Prussians.

Catherine remains strong

After the birth of Paul, many in Elizabeth's court thought that Catherine, now 25 years old, would lead a quiet life with no hope of future power. But they did not know Catherine. She returned to court smiling, proud, and wearing a beautiful blue velvet dress with gold embroidery. She remained as determined as ever to wear Russia's crown. Peter ignored her, so she found other friends who enjoyed her company.

On December 9, 1757, Catherine gave birth to a daughter, Anna. As had happened before, Elizabeth took the baby to her own rooms and left Catherine alone. This time, Catherine was not surprised. Anna died at 18 months of a childhood illness.

A lonely life

Catherine's life was difficult. She missed her children. Her husband ignored her. Her father had died in 1747, and her mother died in 1760.

Elizabeth was no longer kind to Catherine. She accused Catherine of spying to help the king of Prussia. It was not true. Peter was the one helping the Prussians. When Russia went to war against Prussia in 1756 (the Seven Years' War), Peter told Frederick II, king of Prussia, about the Russian war plans. Catherine did not tell Elizabeth about Peter. She simply tried to stay out of Elizabeth's way.

The Seven Years' War

The Seven Years' War (1756–1763) was the first worldwide war. In North America, it was a struggle between France and England over who should control the colonies. In Europe, it was a struggle between Austria and Prussia for power in Germany. Russia sided with Austria in 1757 against the Prussians.

Peter admired Frederick the Great, king of Prussia, even though the Russians were fighting the Prussians during the Seven Years' War. This painting shows Frederick leading his soldiers in battle.

Seizing Power

Gregory Orlov first won fame in the Seven Years' War.

In 1759, Catherine fell in love with Gregory Orlov. By August 1761, she was expecting his child. Gregory was one of five brothers who served in the **Russian Guard**, a special military unit established by Peter the Great. The Orlovs knew that Catherine faced dangers from both Elizabeth and Peter. They were eager to help.

Death of an empress

In 1761, Elizabeth was 52. She was overweight, and her legs were so swollen that she could not walk. Everyone knew her death was near. She died on December 25, 1761, of heart failure.

Elizabeth never got around to making Paul her heir, so Peter was declared emperor. As was the custom at the Russian **court**, the **nobility**, army, representatives of the merchants and craftsmen, and religious leaders swore loyalty to their new emperor. Peter made no secret of his love for Prussia. He expressed his dislike for all things Russian. He irritated Elizabeth's supporters even more when he failed to show proper respect for his dead aunt. On the day of Elizabeth's funeral, Peter clowned around and laughed during the funeral service.

Catherine seemed genuinely upset over Elizabeth's death. Her black dress is a sign of mourning.

Now that he was emperor, Peter ordered that all fighting with Prussia be stopped. The Russian Army was stunned. Peter made matters worse by insisting they wear Prussian uniforms.

Secret child

Catherine kept her pregnancy a secret. If Peter found out, he would divorce her and send her to prison. To keep the child a secret, Catherine pretended to sprain her ankle. She stayed in bed, hiding under the fluffy bed covers. One trusted maid and a male servant, Chkurin, helped her.

On the night of April 11, 1762, Catherine sent her loyal servant, Chkurin, to set fire to his own house. Peter, who loved fires, rushed out to see it. While he was gone, Catherine gave birth to a son. Chkurin hid the child in a beaver fur blanket and took him to a safe house. Catherine barely saw her child before he disappeared.

Alexei, Count Bobrinsky

Catherine named her secret child Alexei after his uncle, Count Alexei Orlov, and Bobrinsky after the estate on which he lived. He lived in the small village of Bobriki, not far from Moscow. In 1781, Catherine sent him a letter admitting that she was his mother. When his half-brother Paul became emperor, he made Alexei a count of the Russian Empire and, later, a major-general. Count Bobrinsky died on June 20, 1813, at the age of 51.

This portrait shows Alexei at about seven years old.

Danger for Catherine

Peter was quick to act on matters of state, but slow to plan his official **coronation**. He seemed to want to delay the ceremony. But as Peter gained confidence, he hinted that he would disinherit his son, Paul, and put Catherine in prison so he would be free to marry someone else. Catherine's supporters knew they must act soon or it would be too late. On June 12, 1762, Peter went to Oranienbaum to rest. He sent Catherine to nearby Peterhof, where he could keep an eye on her. Catherine was fearful, but she knew that when things got too dangerous, the Orlov brothers were ready to act on her behalf.

Overthrowing Peter

On June 28, 1762, one of the Orlov brothers appeared at Peterhof in the middle of the night. He told Catherine it was time to claim the throne before Peter put her in prison. At St. Petersburg, Catherine met with the Russian Guard. They hated Peter and his Prussian ways, but would they support her takeover? Yes! The Guard cheered, knelt down before Catherine, and kissed her cloak. Russia was hers.

That evening Catherine, wearing the uniform of the Russian Guard, confronted Peter. He hid that night. Finally he showed himself the next morning. He did not resist the takeover.

This modern photo shows the interior of Oranienbaum Palace, where Peter went to rest and relax.

Peter's fate

Peter was put in prison. Eight days later, on July 6, 1762, he died, murdered by Russian Guards who supported Catherine. Catherine was horrified. Many assumed that she was responsible, but that was not so. The government reported that Peter died of a stomach ailment. No one cared enough to investigate and discover the truth. Peter's **reign** was over within six months.

Preparing to rule

On the day she took over, Catherine was 33 years old. She had spent over half her life in Russia preparing to rule. Now that the day had arrived, Catherine realized how shaky her position was: there were many enemies at home and abroad ready to challenge her right to rule Russia. On July 7, she announced that her coronation would take place on September 22. She used the time beforehand to build support within the Army and the church. She also gained support from France, Austria, and England.

Overwhelming problems

Catherine met with Russia's Senate, a group of nobles who voted on laws. She learned that Russia was broke, that over 200,000 **peasants** were rebelling by refusing to work, and that Russia lacked good health care. Catherine hoped to make life better for the Russian people.

Catherine had to solve the money problem. She returned her personal allowance to the government. This amount was equal to one-thirteenth of Russia's budget. The Senate wept and cheered at this decision. Next, she printed paper money. In most countries, gold or silver guarantees that the money has real value. However, people had such faith in Catherine that they accepted and used the new money, even though there was no gold or silver to back it up.

Catherine rode among the Russian Guards when she went to St. Petersburg to claim the throne.

A largely unknown country

When Catherine seized power, there were about 20 million people living in Russia. When the Senate announced that each Russian town would have its own military governor, Catherine asked how many towns there were in Russia. No one knew. She sent a young officer to buy an atlas.

ON HER OWN

The **coronation** of Catherine the Great took place in Moscow at the Cathedral of the Assumption. She wore an ermine cloak made of 4,000 animal skins. Her coronation robes were studded with diamonds, pearls, and other precious jewels. She gave the goldsmiths one pound of gold and twenty pounds of silver to make into a crown. She put aside 600,000 **rubles** (silver coins) to toss at the crowd. She even provided a feast of meat, cakes, and wine so that the common people could take part in the celebration. Feasts, fireworks, and balls continued for days.

It took two months to prepare for Catherine's coronation. Seamstresses had to make this beautiful dress. A portrait of Catherine in her later years hangs behind the dress in this photo.

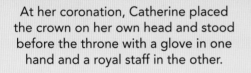

At her coronation, Catherine placed the crown on her own head and stood before the throne with a glove in one hand and a royal staff in the other.

Tireless worker

Power gave Catherine energy and confidence. She felt she could solve Russia's problems, so she woke each morning at five o'clock and worked twelve to fourteen hours a day. She invited foreign leaders and writers to Russia in an effort to spread her own fame beyond the borders of Russia. She also called on Russian doctors, dentists, architects, and engineers living overseas to return home. She would make it possible for them to do business in Russia. She reduced taxes and encouraged foreign trade. She even invited German farmers to move to Russia as a way to increase the population and improve farming.

The Enlightenment

Catherine's **philosophy** reflected her reading of French writers like Voltaire and Diderot. They believed that people must learn to reason freely rather than rely on the government and church to tell them what to think. This 18th-century philosophy was called the **Enlightenment. Enlightened** rulers, like Catherine, tried to make life better for the common people. Nevertheless, Catherine believed in the absolute power of the ruler.

Paul

When Catherine became empress, Paul was 8 years old. Catherine watched over Paul's health and his education, but they were never close. As he grew older, Paul blamed Catherine for his father's death.

The Great Instruction

One of Catherine's first projects was to change Russia's laws to reflect **enlightened** thinking. It was an immense job. Catherine wrote *The Great Instruction*, which contained 655 different **articles**. *The Great Instruction* explained Catherine's desire to reorganize the government of Russia. She also wished to improve the treatment of criminals and protect **peasants** and **serfs**. It was addressed to educated people in Russia and throughout the world.

The Great Instruction was first published in Russian, and then translated into English, Italian, Greek, Swedish, Dutch, Polish, and Romanian.

Smallpox returns

In 1864, **smallpox** returned to Russia. Catherine learned of a method for preventing the disease. It involved taking the pus from a sick person and injecting it into a healthy person. Only one percent of those who were injected died from the disease. Catherine decided to try it herself with the help of a famous London doctor, Thomas Dimsdale. Her advisors begged her not to do it, but Catherine insisted. Everyone waited to see if she would survive. When it was obvious that Catherine remained healthy, others felt confident enough to try it. Her daring saved many lives, and Catherine's fame increased among her people and throughout Europe.

Serfs

Serfs were peasants who worked on farms, in mines, and as servants. Like slaves, they "belonged" to the land or to the noble who owned them. A serf could not own land or attend school. Catherine thought that serfs should be able to own property, but the nobles did not. Catherine often gave both land and serfs to those who helped her. For example, she gave 18,000 male serfs to 40 people who helped her overthrow Peter III. Russian serfs were not freed until 1861, more than 50 years after Catherine's death.

FACING CHALLENGES

On April 28, 1767, Catherine took a trip on the Volga River to learn more about Russia and her people. Eleven specially equipped ships carried Catherine and the 2,000 members of her party. She included high-ranking officials and their wives, foreign **diplomats**, friends, **ladies-in-waiting**, and servants. She stopped at towns and trading centers along the way, touring historic sites, churches, and various factories. She listened to the concerns of nobles, merchants, church officials, and workers. The trip helped her to understand the massive problems ahead as she tried to **reform** (improve) life in Russia. She noticed poor farming practices and poor housing. She realized it was difficult to rule a land of such **diverse** people, religions, and customs.

Trying to fix the laws

The trip took two months. When Catherine returned to Moscow, she called together a Great Commission. This group was made up of 564 representatives from every region of Russia. It was set up to review Russia's laws based on recommendations Catherine had made in the Great Instruction. It was an experiment that failed. The group could not agree on changes. After about a year, Catherine suspended their meetings. The Commission never met again.

Plague

Catherine faced one crisis after another. In 1770, **bubonic plague**, a deadly infection, spread through Russia. The plague continued until December 1771, when a freeze killed the bacteria that caused the plague.

Touring the Volga allowed Catherine to see Russia's natural resources and her people.

Volga River

The Volga River is Europe's longest river and a vital trade link within Russia. It begins in the hills northwest of Moscow and runs 2,193 miles (3,530 kilometers) to the Caspian Sea. The river system includes about 151,000 rivers and streams, with a total length of about 357,000 miles (575,000 kilometers).

Meeting the needs of children

To help Russia's children, Catherine established a home for orphans and a school for midwives (women who help with childbirth). She felt that Russia's strength was in its people, so insuring their health and education was important. By the end of her **reign**, she established about 550 elementary schools. There was at least one high school in each province or region.

Trouble with the neighbors

Catherine also had to deal with two large, rebellious neighbors: Poland and Turkey. Shortly after she came to power, Catherine installed her friend, Stanislas Poniatowski, as king of Poland. When Polish nobles rebelled in 1768, Russia sent troops. The fighting crossed the border into Turkey, and so Turkey declared war on Russia.

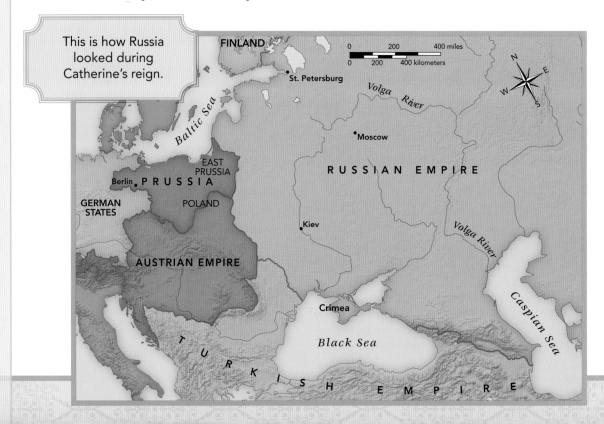

This is how Russia looked during Catherine's reign.

This painting shows Russian troops (in ship at left) claiming the city of Izmail during a war with Turkey.

In 1772, fighting in Poland stopped. Austria, Prussia, and Russia divided Poland, each claiming a third of the Polish land. Fighting with Turkey continued until Turkey agreed to allow Russian ships sailing rights on the Black Sea. It was an uneasy peace. Conflicts with both Poland and Turkey continued throughout Catherine's reign. These wars resulted in Russia gaining more territory and people, just as Catherine had planned.

Rebellion at home

In October 1773, Catherine learned that an Army deserter named Emilian Pugachev had organized a revolt. Soldiers, **serfs**, factory workers, and others from eastern and southern Russia who felt mistreated joined the rebellion. Pugachev convinced the people that he was really Peter III, Catherine's murdered husband. Catherine sent troops to stop the rebels. It took nearly a year to put down Pugachev's rebellion.

Catherine admired Potemkin's abilities as a soldier and leader. He helped gain new territories in Turkey and built Russian cities there.

In love again

By 1770, Catherine no longer felt close to Gregory Orlov. In 1774, she fell in love with Gregory Potemkin. He became one of Catherine's most trusted advisors. Potemkin took command of the new lands won from Turkey in 1774. He established Russian cities, launched a Russian fleet on the Black Sea, and built up the Army. He remained a trusted friend to Catherine until his death in 1791.

A new heir

Catherine arranged a marriage between her son Paul and a German princess in 1773, when Paul was 19. His first wife died before they had children, but Paul married another German princess. They had several children.

Alexander, Paul's first son, became Catherine's favorite. She claimed him at birth, just as Elizabeth had claimed Paul. Now Catherine was the one with the power to do as she wished. Catherine raised the child as her own. She was convinced that Alexander was gifted. She hoped he would become emperor after she died.

Catherine the writer

Catherine wrote almost every day. She wrote political works, like the Great Instruction. She wrote plays, fairy tales, poems, and her **memoirs**. Thousands of pages of her writing still exist today.

Catherine's potatoes

Catherine never tired of suggesting new ideas to the Russian people. For example, she recommended that farmers plant potatoes, which Russians called "ground apples." She wrote instructions on how to cook potatoes and served them at the palace.

The arts

For most of her life, Catherine supported theater and dance. She encouraged the publication of books by Russian and European writers. Catherine was also interested in architecture. She expanded the Alexander Palace in St. Petersburg using simple designs based on Greek architecture. She encouraged the creation of parks and gardens. She had a giant statue of Peter the Great built on the Senate Square.

Catherine had this statue of Peter the Great built as a monument to his **reign**, which she tried to continue.

THE END OF A REIGN

For years the Russians had been claiming land belonging to Turkey. In 1787, the leader of Turkey declared war on Russia. The more skilled Russian troops won the war, but it took four years. In the Treaty of Jassy (1792), Russia gained a large area of land on the Black Sea, as well as the Crimean peninsula (see map page 42).

Growing old

As Catherine grew older, she tired of criticism. She feared that new writers and thinkers would change Russia. In her final years, Catherine closed theaters that put on plays contrary to her ideas. She ordered the burning of books that criticized the **Russian Orthodox** faith.

Catherine did not trust her son Paul. She prepared a secret document declaring her grandson, Alexander, the next emperor. She planned to announce her decision on November 24, 1796.

A sudden death

By age 67, Catherine suffered frequent stomach problems. Her legs were sore and swollen. On the morning of November 5, 1796, she suffered a **stroke**.

Her son Paul rushed to the palace. When he realized that his mother was dying, he tossed many of her official papers into the burning fireplace, including those making Alexander the next emperor. When Catherine II died on November 6, 1796, 42-year-old Paul became Emperor Paul I. Four years later, Paul was murdered and Alexander became emperor.

A remarkable ruler

During the 34 years that Catherine ruled Russia, the Russian Empire added large amounts of land formerly claimed by Poland and Turkey. Catherine reformed the laws and tried to reorganize the government. She also expanded education and supported the arts.

Although Catherine was kind to her supporters and to those who worked with her, she was quick to punish those who rebelled. She did not free the **serfs** nor provide them much relief. However, she helped merchants, craftsmen, and farmers to organize and improve their businesses. This strengthened Russian villages and towns. During Catherine's rule, Russia grew from a little-known and poorly understood nation into a world power.

Catherine loved Russia. She spent her **reign** expanding Russian territory and improving life for the Russian people.

TIMELINES

Catherine's life

APRIL 21, 1729   Sophia Augusta Fredericka of Anhalt-Zerbst (future Catherine the Great) is born in Stettin, Prussia.

1739   Princess Sophie meets Peter Ulrich in Kiel.

1741   Elizabeth becomes empress of Russia and makes Peter her heir.

1744   Sophie and her mother go to Russia (January). They arrive in St. Petersburg in February. Sophie **converts** to **Russian Orthodox** religion and is named Grand Duchess Catherine. She becomes engaged to Grand **Duke** Peter (June).

1745   Catherine marries Peter.

1754   Catherine gives birth to son, Paul.

1757   Catherine gives birth to daughter, Anna.

1759   Daughter Anna dies. Catherine falls in love with Gregory Orlov.

1761   Elizabeth dies. Peter becomes emperor (December).

1762   Son Alexei is born (April). Peter is overthrown and Catherine becomes empress (June). Peter is murdered (July). Catherine is crowned (September).

1764   Catherine is vaccinated against **smallpox**.

1764–66 Catherine writes *The Great Instruction*.

1767 Catherine cruises Volga River. The Great Commission meets.

1768 Turkey declares war on Russia.

1771 Russia conquers the Crimea. There is a plague in Moscow.

1772 Poland is divided. Russia makes peace with Turkey.

1773 War with Turkey. Paul marries. Pugachev rebellion threatens Catherine's rule.

1774 Pugachev rebellion is subdued. Catherine falls in love with Potemkin.

1776 Paul's wife dies; he remarries.

1777 Catherine's first grandson, Alexander, is born. Alliance with Prussia.

1781 Alliance with Austria.

1783 Gregory Orlov dies. Granddaughter Alexandra is born.

1784 Russia takes over Crimea. Granddaughter Helena is born.

1787 War between Russia and Poland.

1791 Potemkin dies.

1792 Russians enter Poland; Treaty ends fighting with Turkey.

1796 Catherine dies. Paul I becomes emperor.

World timeline

1703	City of St. Petersburg founded
1715	Louis XV becomes king of France
1728	Peter III born in Kiel
1732	George Washington, U.S. president born
1740	Frederick II becomes ruler of Prussia
1741	Elizabeth becomes empress of Russia
1742	Prussians conquer the Austrians
1743	Thomas Jefferson, U.S. president, born
1744	France declares war on England and Austria; Prussia invades Saxony and Bohemia
1747	Prussia and Sweden form an alliance
1755	Empress Elizabeth opens the first Russian university
1756	The Seven Years' War begins
1757	British troops occupy Calcutta, India
1758	Thousands killed when Prussian Army defeats Russians at Zorndorf
1759	British Museum opens
1760–1840	Industrial Revolution takes place in England
1764	Treaty between Russia and Prussia to control Poland

1768–74 War between Russia and Turkey

1772 Poland divided among Russia, Austria, and Prussia

1775–83 North American Revolutionary War

1776 Declaration of Independence in North America

1779 Spain declares war on England

1783 Peace treaty signed between England, France, Spain, and the United States.

1786 Frederick the Great dies

1787–91 Russia and Austria wage war against Turkey

1788–90 War between Russia and Sweden

1789 George Washington becomes first President of the United States

1789–99 French Revolution takes place

1792 Treaty of Jassy between Russia and Turkey

1793 France declares war on England, Holland, and Spain; Russia and Prussia divide Poland again; England seizes French settlements in India

1794 Polish revolt stopped by Russia

1795 Secret treaty between Russia and Austria over Poland

GLOSSARY

article piece of writing that is part of a larger book. There were 655 articles in Catherine the Great's Instruction.

bubonic plague deadly disease caused by the bite of an infected rat or flea or contact with an infected person. Bubonic plague killed thousands in Russia.

Catholic Christian church headed by the pope. The Catholic church has its headquarters in Rome.

coat-of-arms shield decorated with the designs of a particular person, family, or institution. Sophie's father owned dishes bearing an image of his coat-of-arms.

convert change religion, opinion, or course of action. Catherine converted to the Russian Orthodox faith.

coronation ceremony of crowning a royal ruler. Catherine wore an elegant dress to her coronation.

court group composed of the family, advisors, and attendants of royalty. Catherine chose her own court.

courtier attendant at a royal court. Courtiers try to please the king and queen.

curtsy greeting made by bending the knees and dipping the body slightly as a sign of respect. As a child, Catherine learned to curtsy.

devout very religious. A devout person may worship every day.

diplomat representative of a government who handles relationships with other governments. Diplomats from several countries served in Catherine's court.

diverse varied or different. We all have diverse interests.

duke prince who rules an independent territory. A duke has power over the people who live in his territory.

enlightened someone who follows the philosophies of the Enlightenment. Catherine was an enlightened ruler.

Enlightenment 18th-century philosophy based on the idea that people must learn to reason freely rather than rely on the government and church to tell them what to think. The Enlightenment began in France.

governess woman who teaches children in a private home. Princess Sophie learned French from her governess.

groom person who looks after horses

lady-in-waiting woman who waits upon a queen or princess. Catherine had several ladies-in-waiting to help her dress for special events.

Lutheran Protestant denomination (branch of a religion) begun by Martin Luther. Prince Christian Augustus was a Lutheran.

memoir story of someone's life that he or she has written. Catherine wrote a memoir.

nobility high rank in society. Princes and princesses are members of the nobility.

peasant poor farm worker

philosophy system of principles (rules) for the conduct of life. Everyone has a philosophy, or set of principles, to guide their life.

pneumonia disease of the lungs that makes it hard to breathe. If untreated, pneumonia can kill.

principality territory ruled by a prince. Prussia consisted of many principalities.

Protestant branch of the Christian faith that broke away from the Roman Catholic church. The Lutheran church is a Protestant church.

reform change or improve. Catherine wanted to reform Russian laws.

Reformation 16th-century religious movement aimed at reforming the Catholic church. The Lutheran church grew out of the Reformation.

reign period of time that a particular king or queen ruled. Catherine's reign lasted 34 years.

ruble silver coin used in Russia. Russian peasants did not earn many rubles.

Russian Guard elite military unit begun by Peter the Great. The Orlov brothers were members of the Russian Guard.

Russian Orthodox national church of Russia. Elizabeth and Catherine attended Russian Orthodox church services.

serf Russian peasant who has no vote, cannot purchase freedom, and cannot get an education. Serfs were similar to slaves, except they had to pay taxes.

smallpox contagious disease that killed 30 to 40 percent of those who caught it. Smallpox has been eliminated thanks to a vaccination program.

stroke sudden illness caused by lack of oxygen to the brain. Catherine died of a stroke.

vain concerned about one's looks or possessions. Someone who looks in the mirror all the time might be vain.

Want to Know More?

Historical note

The popularity of leaders changes over the years. During the last century, Russian historians considered Catherine a foreign ruler who did not care about the Russian people. However, in the 1980s there was a change of attitude. Russian historians began to recognize Catherine's many accomplishments. The first conference to study Catherine's reign was held on the 200th anniversary of her death (1996) in St. Petersburg. Many Russian historians now consider Catherine a great politician who used loyal and capable advisers to manage Russian interests at home and abroad.

Books

Gibson, Karen Bush. *The Life and Times of Catherine the Great*. Hockessin, Del.: Mitchell Lane, 2006.

Gregory, Kristiana. *The Royal Diaries: Catherine: The Great Journey, Russia, 1743*. New York, Scholastic, 2005.

Hatt, Christine. *Catherine the Great*. Milwaukee: World Almanac Library, 2004.

Meltzer, Milton. *Ten Queens: Portraits of Women of Power*. New York: Dutton, 2003.

Whitelaw, Nancy. *Catherine the Great and the Enlightenment in Russia*. Greensboro, North Carolina: Morgan Reynolds Publishing, 2005.

Documentary

Empress of Russia: Catherine the Great (PBS Home Video, 2006).

Website

www.hermitagemuseum.org
Catherine the Great started a royal art collection that later developed into
the Hermitage Museum in St. Petersburg, Russia. The Hermitage, founded
in 1764, contains portraits, dresses, jewelry, games, dishes, and many
other items from Catherine's reign. They can be seen on the website.

Places to visit

Hillwood Estate, Museum & Gardens
4155 Linnean Avenue, NW • Washington, D.C. 20008 • (202) 686-5807
www.hillwoodmuseum.org
Hillwood Estate, Museum & Gardens, Washington, D.C. has one of the
largest collections of Russian Imperial art from the 1700s and 1800s,
outside of Russia. This includes two golden Easter eggs once belonging
to Catherine.

INDEX